W9-AAJ-485

Christmas Moccasins

Christmas Moccasins

Written and illustrated by
Ray Buckley

Abingdon Press

Nashville

Christmas Moccasins

Book design: R. E. Osborne

ISBN 0-687-02738-1

03 04 05 06 07 08 09 10 11 12 – 10 9 8 7 6 5 4 3 2 1

Printed in Hong Kong

To my mother, Josephine

And to my grandmothers and those before them. We do not call them by name. They have made the journey and have new ones. We remember those we love by telling their stories.

We do not forget them.

December moons are never alone. This one, surrounded by ice crystals, embraced the snow with its second-hand light, and coldly shone on the two of us.

My grandmother always wore moccasins. With hardly a sound, they made rounded snow-hugs impressed in the drifts. "How much further," I asked, holding onto her coat. "Not far," she said softly, "not far."

I wondered if the trees remembered us. Remembered that months before we had walked this way. Did they recall that an old woman and a small child had been stopped by three drunken youths? Did the trees remember that those youths had hit us? That they had knocked us down, and, laughing, had taken our coats and my grandmother's moccasins? Would they know that my grandmother had walked home barefoot in the snow, and that frostbite had taken two toes?

Arriving back at my grandmother's house we didn't exchange words. We didn't know what to say. My grandmother boiled water in the teakettle. She poured a cup half full for me, and then poured canned milk into the hot water. While I sat at her table, she filled a basin with water. Softly she unrolled and unbraided her hair, which hung below her knees, in soft shades of white, gray, and black. Her small amber hands splashed water on her upturned face as she lifted her closed eyes toward the ceiling. Carefully she dipped her hands into the basin again and again, patting the length of her hair, her shoulders, her torso, and her legs. In October, with no stream unfrozen, it was her way of cleansing her spirit—the way of beginning something sacred. In the twilight of the kitchen, my grandmother was praying.

*S*he was a remarkable beader. With tiny Czechoslovakian beads so small they strained the eye, she began to make three pair of moccasins. Slowly they emerged, the tops and sides covered in faceted beads of blue, yellow, red, and white. Then, without a thought, she did the unexpected. My grandmother carefully began beading the bottoms of the moccasins, something rarely seen.

November slept and December danced white. Each day the moccasins became more lovely. Christmas Eve came and the moccasins lay on a shelf near the kitchen. Grandmother smoothed out the brown paper saved from the butcher. Carefully each set of moccasins was laid on its own piece of paper and wrapped securely.

Now Grandmother filled the basin with water and dipping her hands into its coolness, quietly patted her warm face, her hair, her shoulders, and her legs. Without a word, she motioned for me to stand by her. She dipped my hands into the water and brought them to my face. I patted my short hair, my shoulders, my legs, as I had seen her do. We put on our coats and stepping out into the snowflakes, which came to greet us, we began to walk.

Pausing at the top of a low hill, she prayed quietly. I could not control the pounding of my heart. "Why are we here?" I asked my grandmother. "Why are we going to see them? On Christmas Eve?" Her shoulders and head were bent toward the snow. There was a long quiet before her words were heard. "We're here to do the Creator's work," she said. "We're here to do the Creator's work."

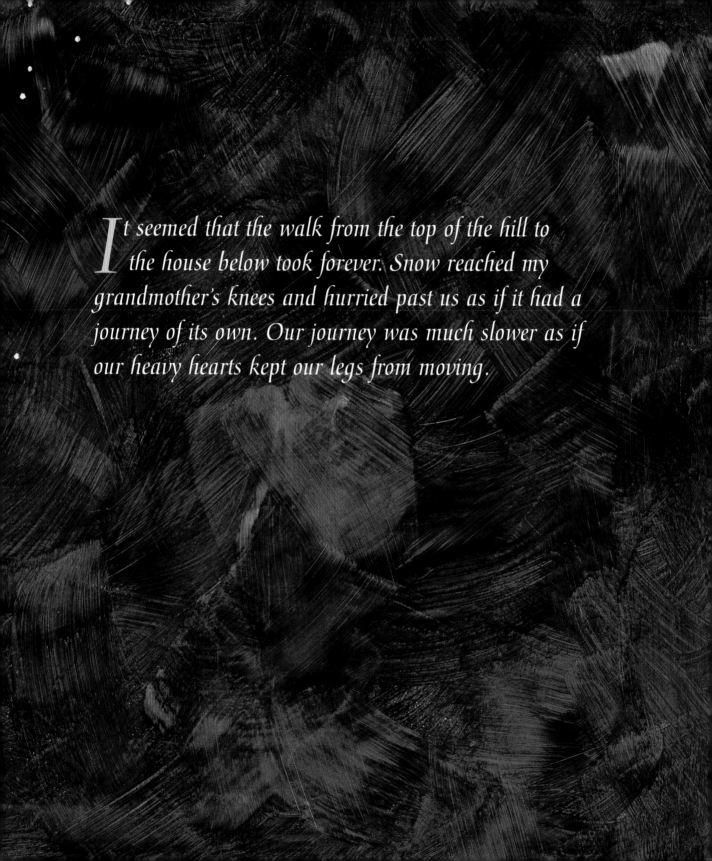

*I*t seemed that the walk from the top of the hill to the house below took forever. Snow reached my grandmother's knees and hurried past us as if it had a journey of its own. Our journey was much slower as if our heavy hearts kept our legs from moving.

*T*he door was opened by a large man. Behind him was a juniper tree covered in Christmas lights. "I have small presents for your sons," my grandmother began. "May I give them?"
She handed each a package carefully wrapped.
To each she said, "I wanted to wish you a Merry Christmas. God bless you."

The room was quiet. Three pair of moccasins lay in three sets of hands; covered in faceted beads in white and red, blue and yellow, they caught the light of the cabin, like the snow caught the light of the moon. There was no need for words. None were spoken.

The moon shone down on an old woman with a
limp and a little boy holding onto her coat.
With shoulders back we smiled at the snow, the trees,
and the world around our feet. At the grove of trees,
my grandmother paused to touch each one,
as if to say, "It's O.K."

In the small house were captives of God's love.
But we were truly free, liberated by the same love.